# The Mindful Pursuit of Wealth

## How to Build a Fulfilling Life with a Balanced Relationship to Money

Oliver George

# Table of contents

# Introduction

**Here's an overview of the book, "The Mindful Pursuit of Wealth**: *How to Build a Fulfilling Life with a Balanced Relationship to Money*":

This book explores the psychological and emotional factors that influence our relationship with money, and how we can cultivate a more mindful and healthy attitude towards wealth. The book draws on the latest research in psychology and behavioral economics to provide insights into why we make the financial decisions we do, and how we can make better choices in the future. It covers topics such as the power of perspective, the emotional traps of greed and envy, the role of luck and chance, and the importance of patience and discipline.

Mary was always good with money. She carefully budgeted her income and saved what she could. But recently, her expenses had started to outpace her income. She was working more and more hours, but she was still falling behind. She started to feel overwhelmed and anxious about money. She didn't know where to turn. Then, she heard about the idea of "mindful money management". She decided to try it. First, she took a step back and examined her relationship with money. She realized that her anxiety about money was affecting her mood, her relationships, and even her health. She decided to take a different approach. She started to focus on what money could do for her, rather than just focusing on what she didn't have. She started setting goals for herself, such as saving for a vacation or paying off her student loans. As she focused on these positive goals, she started to feel more in control of her finances and less anxious about money. She was even able to find ways to enjoy her life while still making progress on her goals.

Mary's story is an example of how the mindful pursuit of wealth can help people improve their relationship with money and find more happiness in their lives. By focusing on positive goals and taking a step back from anxiety, we can start to feel more in control of our financial situation. A more balanced and satisfying existence may result from this. What do you think of Mary's story? Do you think the principles of mindful money management could help you in your own life? Sure!

As Mary continued to apply the principles of mindful money management to her life, she started to see the benefits. She was able to pay off her student loans and save for a vacation. She also started to feel more relaxed and less stressed. Her relationships improved, as she wasn't constantly worrying about money. She even started to take up a new hobby, which gave her more joy in her life. She felt like she had more time for the things she loved, and her overall well-being improved.

All of these benefits added up to a more balanced and fulfilling life. The changes in Mary's life were a result of her commitment to making small, consistent changes in her financial habits. By taking small steps every day, she was able to make a big impact on her overall happiness and well-being.

In the end, the book that she had purchased turned out to be one of the best investments she ever made. It changed her life in ways she never could have imagined. She was grateful for the knowledge and insights she gained, and she continued to use what she had learned to improve her life even further.

What do you think about how the book helped Mary? Do you think it could have the same impact on someone else? Let's imagine that someone else, let's call her Sarah, purchases the same book and reads it cover to cover. Sarah is also struggling with her finances, and feels overwhelmed and stressed out. How do you think reading the book might change Sarah's life?

Let's imagine that Sarah also starts to apply the principles of mindful money management to her life. Over time, she starts to feel more in control of her finances, and she starts to see the benefits of her efforts. Do you think that Sarah's story might end up similar to Mary's? Why or why not?

I think Sarah's story could end up like Mary's, but there are a few factors that might make her experience different. For one thing, Sarah might have different financial challenges than Mary did, so the solutions she finds might be different. Sarah might also have different values and priorities, so the goals she sets for herself might be different. However, I think the core message of mindful money management - that small, consistent changes can lead to big results - would still apply to Sarah's life. What do you think about the factors that might make Sarah's story different from Mary's? Do you think those factors would make it more or less likely for Sarah to experience the same level of success?

I think the factors that make Sarah's situation different from Mary's could go either way. On the one hand, Sarah might face different challenges that make it harder for her to achieve her goals. On the other hand, she might have unique strengths or resources that help her make progress more quickly. In the end, I think it would come down to how much effort Sarah is willing to put in, and how committed she is to making changes in her life.

Do you think everyone has the ability to improve their financial situation, regardless of their circumstances? Why or why not?

I believe that anyone can make positive changes in their financial situation, even if they're starting from a difficult place. However, I also think that some people have more obstacles to overcome than others. For example, someone who is dealing with significant debt or medical bills might have a harder time getting ahead than someone who is starting with a clean slate. That said, I believe that even the most challenging circumstances can be overcome with the right mindset and support. It might just take longer for some people to achieve their goals

To conclude, I would recommend the book, "The Mindful Pursuit of Wealth: How to Build a Fulfilling Life with a Balanced Relationship to Money". This book offers practical advice and a fresh perspective on how to achieve financial success while maintaining a healthy relationship with money. It's a must-read for anyone who wants to improve their financial situation while also living a fulfilling life.

Thank you for reading, and I hope this has been a helpful discussion! If you have any further questions or comments, feel free to ask.

# CHAPTER 1

## The Power of Perspective

The power of perspective is an extraordinary force that shapes our understanding of the world and influences our actions. It serves as a lens through which we interpret events, relationships, and circumstances, ultimately determining our emotional responses and behavioral choices. In the mindful pursuit of wealth, perspective becomes a crucial asset, guiding individuals towards financial success and fulfillment.

Perspective enables individuals to perceive setbacks as opportunities for growth rather than insurmountable obstacles. Instead of viewing financial challenges as barriers to prosperity, those with a resilient perspective see them as valuable lessons to be learned. By reframing setbacks as stepping stones to success, individuals can maintain a positive outlook and remain motivated in their wealth-building endeavors.

Moreover, perspective empowers individuals to recognize the abundance that surrounds them, fostering a sense of gratitude and contentment. Rather than fixating on what they lack, individuals with an abundant perspective appreciate the resources, opportunities, and relationships available to them. This mindset of abundance cultivates a sense of fulfillment and satisfaction, independent of material wealth.

Furthermore, perspective allows individuals to transcend societal norms and conventional wisdom, enabling them to chart their own path to financial success. By questioning traditional beliefs about money and success, individuals can explore alternative strategies and pursue unconventional opportunities. This willingness to think outside the box empowers individuals to forge their own unique journey towards wealth and fulfillment.

In addition, perspective facilitates empathy and compassion towards others, recognizing that wealth is not solely measured by monetary assets but also by the impact we have on the lives of others. By understanding the diverse experiences and circumstances of those around them, individuals can leverage their resources and expertise to uplift others and contribute to the greater good. This compassionate perspective not only enriches the lives of others but also brings a deeper sense of purpose and meaning to one's own pursuit of wealth.

Ultimately, the power of perspective lies in its ability to shape our reality and influence our trajectory towards wealth and fulfillment. By cultivating a resilient, abundant, open-minded, and compassionate perspective, individuals can navigate the complexities of the financial landscape with grace, wisdom, and integrity, ensuring that their pursuit of wealth is not just prosperous but also incredibly satisfying.

## How Your View of the World Can Affect Your Financial Decisions

The way we perceive the world significantly influences our financial decisions, playing a crucial role in our journey towards wealth. Our worldview acts as a filter through which we interpret information, assess risks, and make choices regarding money matters.

Firstly, our mindset towards money shapes our financial decisions. Individuals with a scarcity mindset tend to view money as limited and finite, leading to fear-based decision-making characterized by hoarding, reluctance to invest, and excessive frugality. Conversely, those with an abundance mindset perceive money as abundant and flowing, enabling them to approach financial decisions with confidence, generosity, and a willingness to take calculated risks.

Moreover, our beliefs about success and worthiness impact our financial decisions. Individuals who equate financial success with self-worth may prioritize earning more money at the expense of other aspects of their lives, leading to workaholism, burnout, and a perpetual cycle of chasing external validation. On the other hand, those who prioritize holistic well-being and fulfillment may make financial decisions that align with their values, such as pursuing meaningful work, investing in experiences, and prioritizing work-life balance.

Furthermore, our attitudes towards risk influence our financial decisions. Risk-averse individuals may shy away from investment opportunities, opting for safer but lower-yielding assets out of fear of losing money. In contrast, risk-tolerant individuals may embrace volatility and uncertainty, recognizing that calculated risks are essential for wealth accumulation and growth. Finding the right balance between risk and reward is crucial in making sound financial decisions that align with one's goals and comfort level.

Additionally, our social and cultural influences shape our financial decisions. Family upbringing, societal expectations, and cultural norms play a significant role in shaping our attitudes towards money, influencing our spending habits, saving behaviors, and investment preferences. Being mindful of these influences allows individuals to critically evaluate their financial decisions and make choices that reflect their own values and aspirations rather than external pressures or expectations.

In essence, our view of the world deeply impacts our financial decisions, guiding our behavior and shaping our financial outcomes. By cultivating a mindful perspective that emphasizes abundance, holistic well-being, risk-awareness, and authenticity, individuals can make financial decisions that align with their values, goals, and aspirations, paving the way for a fulfilling and prosperous journey towards wealth.

# CHAPTER 2

## Understanding Greed and Envy

Understanding greed and envy is essential in the mindful pursuit of wealth, as these emotions can significantly impact our financial decisions and overall well-being. Greed is the insatiable desire for more wealth or possessions, often accompanied by a disregard for ethical considerations or the well-being of others. It manifests as a relentless pursuit of accumulation, driven by a fear of scarcity or a need for external validation.

Greed can lead individuals to engage in risky or unethical behavior, such as fraud, exploitation, or excessive risk-taking in financial markets. It blinds individuals to the true sources of happiness and fulfillment, leading to a never-ending cycle of acquisition and dissatisfaction. Moreover, greed can strain relationships, erode trust, and damage one's reputation, ultimately undermining long-term success and happiness.

Envy, on the other hand, is the resentment or covetousness towards others' possessions, achievements, or advantages. It arises from a sense of inadequacy or comparison, fueling feelings of bitterness, resentment, and inferiority. Envy can distort one's perception of reality, leading to unhealthy competition, social comparison, and a constant craving for validation or status.

Both greed and envy stem from a scarcity mindset, rooted in the belief that there is not enough wealth or success to go around. They feed off each other, creating a toxic cycle of desire, comparison, and discontent. However, cultivating awareness and practicing mindfulness can help individuals transcend these destructive emotions and cultivate a more balanced and fulfilling relationship with wealth.

By shifting towards an abundance mindset, individuals can recognize the inherent abundance in their lives and appreciate the wealth and opportunities available to them. This mindset fosters gratitude, contentment, and generosity, enabling individuals to derive greater satisfaction from what they have rather than constantly craving more.

Moreover, practicing empathy and compassion towards others can help mitigate envy and foster a sense of interconnectedness and goodwill. Instead of viewing others' success as a threat or source of envy, individuals can celebrate their achievements and learn from their experiences, fostering collaboration, mutual support, and collective growth.

In the mindful pursuit of wealth, it is essential to recognize and transcend the destructive influence of greed and envy. By cultivating awareness, practicing gratitude, and fostering compassion, individuals can cultivate a healthier relationship with wealth, grounded in authenticity, integrity, and holistic well-being.

## The Emotional Traps That Can Lead to Financial Missteps

Navigating the landscape of wealth accumulation can be fraught with emotional traps that can lead to financial missteps if not recognized and managed effectively. These emotional pitfalls often stem from deep-seated beliefs, fears, and desires that influence our financial decisions in subtle yet profound ways.

One such trap is the allure of instant gratification. In a culture driven by consumerism and immediate pleasures, the desire for instant gratification can lead individuals to prioritize short-term indulgence over long-term financial stability. This mindset fosters impulsive spending, excessive borrowing, and a lack of foresight, ultimately hindering wealth accumulation and financial security.

Another common emotional trap is the fear of missing out (FOMO). This pervasive feeling of anxiety and inadequacy stems from comparing oneself to others and feeling compelled to keep up with their perceived successes or lifestyles. FOMO can lead individuals to make rash investment decisions, chase speculative trends, or overspend in an effort to maintain appearances, often resulting in financial losses and regret.

Moreover, the fear of failure can paralyze individuals and prevent them from taking necessary risks or pursuing opportunities for growth. This fear of failure can manifest as perfectionism, procrastination, or avoidance of financial planning and investment. By succumbing to this emotional trap, individuals miss out on valuable learning experiences and opportunities for wealth accumulation.

Additionally, the emotional trap of scarcity mindset can distort one's perception of abundance and undermine their confidence in their ability to create wealth. This mindset is characterized by feelings of lack, insecurity, and a constant fear of not having enough. It can lead individuals to hoard resources, avoid investment opportunities, or engage in self-sabotaging behaviors out of fear of scarcity.

Furthermore, the emotional trap of overconfidence can blind individuals to the risks and limitations of their financial decisions, leading to reckless behavior and overestimation of their abilities. Overconfidence can lead individuals to ignore warning signs, underestimate market volatility, or overextend themselves financially, ultimately leading to costly mistakes and financial setbacks.

In the mindful pursuit of wealth, it is essential to recognize and navigate these emotional traps with awareness and resilience. By cultivating emotional intelligence, practicing self-awareness, and seeking support when needed, individuals can make more informed and intentional financial decisions that align with their long-term goals and values.

# CHAPTER 3

# The Impact of Luck and Chance

In the journey towards wealth, the impact of luck and chance cannot be overlooked. While hard work, diligence, and strategic planning are crucial elements of success, external factors beyond our control also play a significant role in shaping our financial outcomes.

Luck and chance can manifest in various forms, from unexpected windfalls and fortunate opportunities to unforeseen setbacks and challenges. For some individuals, being in the right place at the right time or encountering influential connections can open doors to lucrative ventures or career advancements. Conversely, others may experience setbacks or financial losses due to factors beyond their control, such as economic downturns, natural disasters, or personal crises.

The influence of luck and chance highlights the importance of humility and gratitude in the pursuit of wealth. Recognizing the role that external factors play in our success can humble us and prevent us from becoming overly confident or complacent. It reminds us to acknowledge the contributions of others, appreciate the opportunities we receive, and remain mindful of the interconnectedness of our lives.

Moreover, the impact of luck and chance underscores the importance of resilience and adaptability in navigating the uncertainties of life. While we cannot control the hand we are dealt, we can control how we respond to adversity and challenges. Cultivating resilience allows us to bounce back from setbacks, learn from our experiences, and emerge stronger and wiser in the pursuit of our goals.

Furthermore, the recognition of luck and chance can foster empathy and compassion towards others who may not have been as fortunate in their circumstances. It reminds us of the inherent unpredictability of life and the importance of extending support and understanding to those facing difficulties or setbacks.

In the mindful pursuit of wealth, acknowledging the role of luck and chance encourages us to approach our financial goals with a balanced perspective. While we strive for success through hard work and determination, we also recognize the influence of external factors beyond our control. By embracing humility, resilience, and empathy, we can navigate the complexities of life with grace and integrity, regardless of the hand we are dealt.

## How the Unexpected Can Affect Your Financial Journey

The financial journey is often marked by unexpected twists and turns that can significantly impact one's trajectory towards wealth. These unexpected events, whether positive or negative, can disrupt plans, challenge assumptions, and require individuals to adapt and make strategic decisions in response.

On the positive side, unexpected windfalls such as inheritances, bonuses, or sudden business opportunities can accelerate one's progress towards financial goals. However, without careful planning and mindfulness, these windfalls can also lead to impulsive spending, lifestyle inflation, or unsustainable investments. Therefore, it's crucial to approach unexpected wealth with caution, gratitude, and a long-term perspective, ensuring that it is used wisely to support one's financial well-being and long-term goals.

Conversely, unexpected setbacks such as job loss, medical emergencies, or market downturns can derail even the most carefully laid financial plans. These challenges can test one's resilience, requiring individuals to reassess priorities, cut expenses, and seek alternative sources of income. While such setbacks can be disheartening, they also present opportunities for growth, learning, and resourcefulness. By remaining flexible, proactive, and resilient, individuals can navigate unexpected challenges and emerge stronger and more resilient in their financial journey.

Moreover, unexpected life events such as marriage, divorce, childbirth, or relocation can also have significant financial implications, impacting expenses, income, and long-term financial goals. These transitions require individuals to adapt their financial strategies, update estate planning documents, and consider the financial implications of major life decisions. By approaching these transitions with mindfulness and foresight, individuals can ensure that they remain on track towards their financial goals while navigating life's inevitable changes.

In summary, the unexpected can profoundly influence one's financial journey, presenting both opportunities and challenges along the way. By cultivating mindfulness, resilience, and adaptability, individuals can navigate these unexpected twists and turns with grace and integrity, ensuring that they remain on course towards their financial goals despite the uncertainties of life.

# CHAPTER 4

# The Role of Patience and Discipline

In the pursuit of wealth, patience and discipline play pivotal roles, serving as guiding principles that underpin long-term success and fulfillment. Patience is the ability to tolerate delays, setbacks, and uncertainties without becoming disheartened or impulsive. It entails maintaining a steadfast commitment to one's goals and vision, even in the face of obstacles or slow progress.

Discipline, on the other hand, is the practice of self-control, consistency, and perseverance in the pursuit of one's objectives. It involves making deliberate choices, adhering to a plan or strategy, and resisting the temptation of short-term gratification in favor of long-term gains.

Together, patience and discipline form the cornerstone of a mindful approach to wealth accumulation, shaping individuals' behaviors, attitudes, and decisions in profound ways. Here's how:

1. **Patience fosters a long-term perspective:** In a world characterized by instant gratification and immediate results, patience allows individuals to adopt a broader view of their financial journey. Rather than seeking quick fixes or overnight success, patient individuals understand that true wealth is built gradually over time through consistent effort, resilience, and perseverance.

2. **Discipline ensures consistency and accountability**: Discipline provides the structure and accountability needed to stay on track towards financial goals. It helps individuals establish healthy habits, such as budgeting, saving, and investing regularly, and stick to them even when faced with distractions or temptations. By adhering to a disciplined

approach, individuals can make steady progress towards their objectives and avoid succumbing to impulsive or irrational decisions.

3. **Patience and discipline mitigate risks**: In the volatile world of finance, patience and discipline act as buffers against irrational behavior and excessive risk-taking. Patient investors understand the importance of diversification, risk management, and staying the course during market fluctuations. Similarly, disciplined savers prioritize building emergency funds, paying off debt, and avoiding unnecessary expenses, thereby reducing financial vulnerabilities and mitigating potential losses.

4. Patience and discipline foster resilience: Financial success is often accompanied by setbacks, failures, and unexpected challenges. However, individuals who cultivate patience and discipline are better equipped to weather these storms with resilience and grace. They view setbacks as temporary obstacles rather than insurmountable barriers, learning from their

experiences and adapting their strategies accordingly.

In essence, patience and discipline are essential virtues that empower individuals to navigate the complexities of the financial landscape with wisdom, integrity, and resilience. By cultivating these qualities, individuals can achieve not only financial success but also greater fulfillment, peace of mind, and well-being on their journey towards wealth.

## How Self-Control Can Help You Reach Your Financial Goals

Self-control is a potent tool in the arsenal of those aiming to achieve their financial goals. It acts as a guiding force, enabling individuals to make prudent decisions, resist impulsive temptations, and stay focused on their long-term objectives. Here's how self-control can pave the way to financial success:

1. **Budgeting and Spending Control**: Self-control empowers individuals to create and stick to a budget, allocating their resources wisely and prioritizing spending in alignment with their financial goals. By exercising restraint and avoiding unnecessary expenses, individuals can ensure that their money is directed towards activities that contribute to their long-term financial well-being.

2. **Saving and Investing Discipline**: Self-control is essential in building a habit of regular saving and disciplined investing. It enables individuals to set aside a portion of their income for savings and investments, even when faced with the temptation to splurge or indulge in instant gratification. Consistent saving and investing over time can lead to the accumulation of wealth and the realization of financial goals.

3. **Debt Management**: Self-control plays a crucial role in managing debt effectively. It encourages individuals to avoid taking on excessive debt and to make timely payments to reduce existing debt burdens. By exercising restraint in borrowing and maintaining discipline in debt repayment, individuals can avoid the pitfalls of debt accumulation and maintain a healthy financial position.

4. **Resisting Impulsive Decisions**: Self-control helps individuals resist impulsive decisions that may derail their financial progress. Whether it's resisting the urge to make speculative investments, succumbing to peer pressure to overspend, or giving in to the allure of instant gratification, self-control enables individuals to pause, evaluate their options, and make informed choices that align with their long-term goals.

5. **Emotional Regulation**: Self-control allows individuals to regulate their emotions, particularly during times of financial stress or

uncertainty. By maintaining a calm and rational mindset, individuals can avoid making decisions driven by fear, greed, or other negative emotions that may lead to financial missteps. Instead, they can approach challenges with resilience and clarity, finding constructive solutions to overcome obstacles.

In the mindful pursuit of wealth, self-control serves as a cornerstone, enabling individuals to navigate the complexities of the financial landscape with prudence, discipline, and integrity. By cultivating self-control and harnessing its power, individuals can take control of their financial destiny, make progress towards their goals, and ultimately achieve greater financial security and freedom.

# CHAPTER 5

# The Importance of Humility and Gratitude

In the pursuit of wealth, humility and gratitude serve as essential virtues that contribute to both financial success and personal fulfillment. These qualities foster a mindset of openness, appreciation, and humility, guiding individuals towards a more mindful and balanced approach to wealth accumulation.

Humility reminds individuals of their inherent limitations and the contributions of others to their success. It encourages individuals to acknowledge their strengths and weaknesses, seek guidance and support when needed, and remain open to learning and growth. In the context of wealth accumulation, humility discourages arrogance and entitlement, promoting a more grounded and authentic relationship with money and success.

Gratitude, on the other hand, cultivates a sense of appreciation and contentment for the abundance in one's life. It encourages individuals to recognize and acknowledge the blessings, opportunities, and privileges they enjoy, regardless of their financial status. Gratitude fosters a positive outlook and resilience, even in the face of challenges or setbacks, allowing individuals to find joy and satisfaction in the present moment rather than constantly striving for more.

Together, humility and gratitude provide a solid foundation for the mindful pursuit of wealth by fostering the following:

1. **Financial Responsibility**: Humility encourages individuals to approach wealth with a sense of responsibility and stewardship, recognizing the importance of using their resources wisely and ethically. Gratitude

reinforces this mindset by promoting conscientiousness and appreciation for the opportunities afforded by financial abundance.

2. **Generosity and Giving**: Humility and gratitude inspire individuals to share their wealth and resources with others in need. Whether through charitable donations, volunteer work, or acts of kindness, individuals who cultivate humility and gratitude recognize the importance of giving back to their communities and making a positive impact on the lives of others.

3. **Resilience and Perspective**: Humility and gratitude foster resilience by encouraging individuals to maintain perspective and resilience in the face of financial challenges or setbacks. Rather than dwelling on setbacks or failures, individuals with a humble and grateful mindset are better equipped to learn from their experiences, adapt to changing circumstances, and persevere towards their goals with grace and integrity.

4. **Healthy Relationships**: Humility and gratitude contribute to the cultivation of healthy relationships, both within and outside the realm of finance. By fostering humility, individuals can avoid the pitfalls of ego-driven behavior and maintain authentic connections with others. Gratitude, meanwhile, enhances interpersonal relationships by promoting appreciation, empathy, and mutual respect.

Certainly! Let's delve further into the importance of humility and gratitude in the context of the mindful pursuit of wealth:

5. **Mindful Decision-Making**: Humility and gratitude encourage individuals to approach financial decisions with mindfulness and discernment. Instead of being driven by ego, status, or external validation, individuals with a humble and grateful mindset are more likely to make decisions that align with their values, priorities, and long-term goals. This mindful approach to decision-making minimizes impulsivity and regret, leading to more sustainable and fulfilling outcomes.

6. **Cultivation of Abundance Mentality**: Humility and gratitude cultivate an abundance mentality, which is the belief that there is always enough wealth and resources to go around. Rather than viewing wealth as a finite pie where one person's gain comes at another's expense, individuals with an abundance mindset celebrate the success of others and recognize that opportunities for growth and prosperity are limitless. This mindset fosters collaboration, cooperation, and collective upliftment, benefiting both individuals and society as a whole.

7. **Personal Growth and Fulfillment**: Humility and gratitude contribute to personal growth and fulfillment by fostering introspection, self-awareness, and emotional resilience. Individuals who cultivate these qualities are more likely to engage in continuous self-improvement, seek feedback, and embrace challenges as opportunities for growth. This growth mindset enables individuals to derive

fulfillment from the journey of wealth accumulation itself, rather than solely focusing on the end goal of financial success.

8. **Legacy and Impact**: Humility and gratitude inspire individuals to consider the broader impact of their actions and decisions on future generations and society as a whole. By recognizing the interconnectedness of all beings and the importance of leaving a positive legacy, individuals with a humble and grateful mindset are motivated to make choices that contribute to the greater good and leave a lasting impact beyond their own lifetimes.

In conclusion, humility and gratitude are integral aspects of the mindful pursuit of wealth, shaping individuals' attitudes, behaviors, and relationships in profound ways. By cultivating these qualities, individuals can approach wealth accumulation with integrity, mindfulness, and a sense of purpose, ultimately leading to greater financial success, personal fulfillment, and positive impact on the world around them.

A humble mindset can serve as a powerful guiding force in the pursuit of wealth, steering individuals towards sustainable success, fulfillment, and positive impact. Here's how a humble mindset can lead:

1. **Openness to Learning**: A humble mindset fosters an attitude of openness to learning and growth. Instead of being closed off or resistant to new ideas, individuals with humility embrace opportunities for learning from others, seeking feedback, and continuously improving themselves. This openness to learning enables individuals to stay adaptable and responsive to changing circumstances in the ever-evolving landscape of wealth accumulation.

2. **Collaboration and Teamwork**: Humility promotes collaboration and teamwork,

recognizing that no individual achieves success in isolation. Individuals with a humble mindset are willing to collaborate with others, leverage their strengths, and seek support when needed. By fostering a culture of collaboration and mutual respect, a humble mindset enables individuals to achieve greater collective success than they could alone.

3. **Respect for Others**: A humble mindset cultivates respect for others, regardless of their background, status, or wealth. Rather than seeking to elevate oneself at the expense of others, individuals with humility recognize the inherent worth and dignity of all individuals. This respect fosters positive relationships, trust, and goodwill, laying the foundation for meaningful connections and collaborative endeavors.

4. **Gratitude and Contentment**: Humility encourages individuals to cultivate gratitude and contentment for the blessings and opportunities in their lives. Rather than constantly striving for

more or comparing themselves to others, individuals with humility appreciate what they have and find joy in the present moment. This gratitude and contentment provide a sense of fulfillment and inner peace that transcends material wealth.

5. **Ethical and Responsible Leadership**: Humility is integral to ethical and responsible leadership, as it encourages leaders to prioritize the well-being of others and the greater good over personal gain or ego. Humble leaders lead by example, demonstrating integrity, authenticity, and empathy in their actions and decisions. This ethical leadership fosters trust, loyalty, and sustainability, benefiting both individuals and organizations in the pursuit of shared goals.

In summary, a humble mindset can lead individuals towards greater success, fulfillment, and positive impact in the pursuit of wealth. By fostering openness to learning, collaboration, respect for others, gratitude, and ethical leadership, humility empowers individuals to navigate the complexities of the financial landscape with integrity, mindfulness, and a sense of purpose.

# CHAPTER 6

# Practical strategies for wealth and happiness

Practical strategies for achieving both wealth and happiness involve a balanced approach that integrates financial success with personal well-being. Here are some strategies to consider:

1. **Set Clear Financial Goals**: Start by defining clear and specific financial goals that align with your values and priorities. Whether it's saving for retirement, buying a home, or starting a business, having concrete goals provides direction and motivation for your wealth-building efforts.

2. **Create a Budget and Stick to It**: Develop a budget that outlines your income, expenses, and savings goals. Be realistic about

your spending habits and identify areas where you can cut back or eliminate unnecessary expenses. Sticking to a budget helps you live within your means and prioritize saving and investing for the future.

3. **Diversify Your Income Streams**: Instead of relying solely on a single source of income, consider diversifying your income streams to reduce risk and increase financial stability. This could involve starting a side hustle, investing in real estate, or building passive income streams through investments.

4. **Invest Wisely**: Take a mindful approach to investing by educating yourself about different investment options and assessing their risk and return potential. Diversify your investment portfolio to spread risk across different asset classes, such as stocks, bonds, and real estate. To create an investing plan that suits your objectives and risk tolerance, think about collaborating with a financial advisor.

5. **Practice Frugality and Minimalism**: Embrace frugality and minimalism as guiding principles in your financial life. Focus on living below your means, avoiding unnecessary purchases, and prioritizing experiences and relationships over material possessions. Cultivating a minimalist lifestyle not only saves money but also fosters contentment and happiness.

6. **Cultivate Gratitude and Mindfulness**: Take time each day to cultivate gratitude and mindfulness in your life. Practice gratitude by acknowledging and appreciating the blessings and abundance in your life, whether big or small. Incorporate mindfulness practices such as meditation, deep breathing, or journaling to reduce stress, increase self-awareness, and enhance overall well-being.

7. **Invest in Experiences and Relationships**: Instead of solely focusing on accumulating material possessions, invest in experiences and relationships that bring meaning

and fulfillment to your life. Spend time with loved ones, travel to new places, and pursue hobbies and interests that enrich your life and create lasting memories.

8. **Give Back to Others**: Find ways to give back to your community and make a positive impact on the world around you. Whether through volunteering, charitable donations, or supporting causes you believe in, giving back not only benefits others but also brings a sense of fulfillment and purpose to your own life.

By incorporating these practical strategies into your financial journey, you can achieve both wealth and happiness in a mindful and balanced way. Remember that true wealth is not just about accumulating money and possessions, but about living a life of purpose, meaning, and fulfillment.

# Creating a budget and tracking your spending

Creating a budget and tracking your spending are essential steps in managing your finances effectively and achieving your financial goals. Here's how to approach each aspect:

1. **Creating a Budget**:
   - Start by determining your total monthly income, including wages, salaries, bonuses, and any other sources of income.
   - Next, list all your monthly expenses, including fixed expenses such as rent or mortgage payments, utilities, insurance, and loan payments, as well as variable expenses such as groceries, dining out, entertainment, and transportation.
   - Differentiate between essential expenses (needs) and discretionary expenses (wants) to prioritize your spending.

- Set specific financial goals, such as saving for emergencies, paying off debt, or investing for the future, and allocate funds towards each goal within your budget.
- Ensure that your total expenses do not exceed your total income, and make adjustments as needed to achieve a balanced budget.

2. **Tracking Your Spending**:
- Keep track of every expense you incur, no matter how small, using a method that works for you, such as a smartphone app, spreadsheet, or pen and paper.
- Categorize your expenses to gain insights into your spending patterns and identify areas where you may be overspending or where you can cut back.
- Review your spending regularly, ideally on a weekly or monthly basis, to stay on track with your budget and make any necessary adjustments.

- Be honest and accurate in recording your expenses, and don't forget to include irregular or one-time expenses, such as medical bills or car repairs.
- Use tools and technology to simplify the process, such as automatic expense tracking apps or linking your bank accounts to budgeting software.

By creating a budget and tracking your spending, you gain a clear understanding of your financial situation, identify areas for improvement, and make informed decisions about your money. These practices empower you to take control of your finances, prioritize your goals, and ultimately achieve greater financial stability and success.

## Finding ways to increase your income

Finding ways to increase your income can significantly improve your financial situation and help you achieve your financial goals faster. Here are some strategies to consider:

1. **Negotiate a Raise or Promotion**: If you're currently employed, consider negotiating a raise or seeking a promotion within your company. Highlight your contributions, skills, and achievements to demonstrate your value to your employer and justify a salary increase.

2. **Develop Marketable Skills**: Invest in developing new skills or enhancing existing ones that are in demand in your industry. This could involve taking courses, obtaining certifications, or gaining relevant work experience to make yourself more valuable and marketable to employers.

3. **Freelancing or Consulting**: Explore opportunities for freelancing or consulting in your area of expertise. This could involve offering your services on freelance platforms, networking with potential clients, or reaching

out to companies in need of your skills on a project basis.

4. **Start a Side Business**: Consider starting a side business or pursuing a passion project that has the potential to generate additional income. This could range from selling handmade crafts or products online to offering services such as tutoring, coaching, or freelance writing.

5. **Invest in Real Estate**: Explore opportunities for real estate investment, such as purchasing rental properties or investing in real estate investment trusts (REITs). Real estate can provide a steady stream of passive income and potential for long-term appreciation.

6. **Invest in Stocks or Dividend-Paying Assets**: Invest in stocks, mutual funds, or dividend-paying assets that have the potential to generate passive income through dividends or capital gains over time. For assistance in creating an investing plan that fits your

objectives and risk tolerance, think about consulting with a financial advisor.

7. **Monetize Your Hobbies or Talents**: Identify ways to monetize your hobbies or talents by offering products or services to others. Whether it's teaching music lessons, selling handmade crafts, or offering photography services, there may be opportunities to turn your passions into sources of income.

8. **Explore Remote Work Opportunities**: With the rise of remote work, explore opportunities to work remotely for companies or clients located outside your local area. Remote work can offer flexibility and potentially higher earning potential, especially if you have specialized skills that are in demand globally.

By exploring these strategies and taking proactive steps to increase your income, you can create additional financial opportunities and accelerate your journey towards financial success and security. Remember to assess each opportunity carefully, consider the potential risks and rewards, and make informed decisions that align with your long-term financial goals.

## Living within your means and avoiding debt

Living within your means and avoiding debt are fundamental principles of sound financial management that can lead to long-term financial stability and peace of mind. Here's how to embrace these practices:

1. **Create a Realistic Budget**: Start by assessing your income and expenses to create a realistic budget that aligns with your financial goals and priorities. Differentiate between essential expenses (such as housing, utilities, groceries) and discretionary expenses (such as

dining out, entertainment) to ensure that your spending is in line with your income.

2. **Track Your Spending**: Keep track of your expenses to ensure that you're staying within your budget and not overspending. This could involve using budgeting apps, spreadsheets, or simply keeping receipts and recording expenses manually. Regularly reviewing your spending habits can help identify areas where you may need to cut back or adjust your budget.

3. **Avoid Impulse Purchases**: Practice mindful spending by avoiding impulse purchases and taking time to consider whether a purchase is necessary and aligned with your financial goals. Before making a purchase, ask yourself if it's something you truly need or if it's just a want. Consider implementing a "cooling-off" period for large purchases to prevent impulse buying.

4. **Build an Emergency Fund**: Prioritize building an emergency fund to cover unexpected expenses or financial emergencies, such as medical bills, car repairs, or job loss. Aim to save enough to cover three to six months' worth of living expenses in a separate savings account that is easily accessible in case of emergencies.

5. **Pay Off Debt Strategically**: If you have existing debt, prioritize paying it off strategically by focusing on high-interest debt first, such as credit card debt. Consider using the debt avalanche or debt snowball method to systematically pay off debt while minimizing interest payments. Make consistent payments each month to chip away at your debt and avoid accumulating additional interest.

6. **Live Below Your Means**: Embrace a lifestyle of frugality and simplicity by living below your means and avoiding lifestyle inflation. Instead of constantly upgrading your lifestyle with each increase in income, focus on saving and investing for the future. Adopting a

minimalist mindset can help you prioritize experiences, relationships, and personal fulfillment over material possessions.

7. **Seek Financial Education and Support**: Educate yourself about personal finance and seek guidance from financial advisors, books, online resources, or workshops to improve your financial literacy and make informed decisions about your money. Surround yourself with supportive friends and family who share your financial values and goals.

By living within your means and avoiding debt, you can achieve greater financial freedom, security, and peace of mind. These practices lay the foundation for building wealth, achieving your financial goals, and living a fulfilling and meaningful life. Remember that financial success is not just about how much you earn, but how wisely you manage and allocate your resources.

Prioritizing your needs and wants is a fundamental aspect of responsible financial management and can help you achieve greater financial stability and peace of mind. Here's how to approach prioritization effectively:

1. **Distinguish Between Needs and Wants**:
   - Needs are essential expenses required for survival and basic well-being, such as food, shelter, clothing, healthcare, and transportation.
   - Wants, on the other hand, are discretionary expenses that are not essential for survival but may enhance your quality of life or provide enjoyment, such as dining out, entertainment, travel, and luxury items.

2. **Assess Your Financial Situation**:

- Take stock of your income, expenses, and financial goals to gain a clear understanding of your financial situation.
- Determine your fixed expenses (needs) and variable expenses (wants) to identify areas where you may need to adjust your spending.

3. **Prioritize Your Needs**:

- Start by prioritizing your needs to ensure that essential expenses are covered before allocating funds to discretionary spending.
- Allocate a portion of your income towards essential needs such as housing, utilities, groceries, healthcare, and transportation.
- Consider setting up automatic payments or allocating funds for needs in a separate account to ensure that they are prioritized and paid consistently.

4. **Evaluate Your Wants**:

- Once your needs are covered, evaluate your wants and prioritize them based on their importance, value, and alignment with your financial goals.
- Identify discretionary expenses that bring you the most joy and satisfaction and allocate funds towards those priorities.
- Be mindful of indulging in unnecessary or excessive wants that may strain your budget or detract from your long-term financial goals.

5. **Practice Moderation and Balance**:

- Strive to strike a balance between satisfying your needs and fulfilling your wants, practicing moderation and restraint when it comes to discretionary spending.
- Set limits on discretionary spending and avoid impulse purchases by taking time to consider whether a purchase aligns with your values and financial priorities.

- Be open to adjusting your spending priorities over time as your financial situation and goals evolve.

6. **Revisit and Adjust Regularly**:
- Regularly review and adjust your spending priorities to ensure that they align with your changing circumstances, goals, and values.
- Be flexible and willing to make trade-offs between needs and wants as necessary to stay within your budget and achieve your financial objectives.

By prioritizing your needs and wants, you can make informed decisions about how to allocate your resources in a way that promotes financial well-being, fulfillment, and peace of mind. By focusing on meeting your essential needs first and then allocating funds towards discretionary wants, you can achieve greater financial stability and work towards your long-term goals with confidence.

Managing your emotions and staying motivated are crucial skills in the pursuit of financial goals and overall well-being. Here are some strategies to effectively manage your emotions and maintain motivation:

1. **Cultivate Self-Awareness**: Start by developing self-awareness of your emotions, thoughts, and behaviors related to money. Notice how you feel when making financial decisions, and identify any patterns or triggers that may lead to emotional reactions. By understanding your emotions, you can better manage them and make more rational decisions.

2. **Practice Emotional Regulation**: Learn techniques to regulate your emotions when faced

with financial challenges or setbacks. This could include deep breathing exercises, mindfulness meditation, or positive self-talk. By calming your mind and body, you can approach financial decisions with clarity and perspective.

3. **Set Clear Goals**: Define clear and achievable financial goals that inspire and motivate you. Break down larger goals into smaller, manageable tasks, and celebrate your progress along the way. Having a clear sense of purpose and direction can help you stay focused and motivated, even during difficult times.

4. **Focus on Positivity and Gratitude**: Cultivate a positive mindset by focusing on gratitude and appreciation for what you have, rather than dwelling on what you lack. Practice gratitude exercises such as keeping a gratitude journal or reflecting on three things you're grateful for each day. By shifting your focus towards the positive aspects of your life, you can maintain a sense of optimism and resilience.

5. **Visualize Success**: Visualize yourself achieving your financial goals and imagine how it would feel to accomplish them. Create a vision board or use visualization techniques to vividly imagine your desired outcomes. By visualizing success, you can stay motivated and maintain momentum towards your goals, even when faced with obstacles.

6. **Seek Support and Accountability**: Surround yourself with supportive friends, family members, or mentors who can provide encouragement, advice, and accountability. Share your financial goals with others and enlist their support in staying motivated and accountable. Consider joining a financial support group or hiring a financial coach to provide guidance and accountability.

7. **Celebrate Small Wins**: Acknowledge and celebrate your achievements, no matter how small. Each step forward, no matter how incremental, brings you closer to your goals. Reward yourself for reaching milestones along

the way, whether it's treating yourself to a small indulgence or taking time to relax and recharge.

8. **Stay Flexible and Adapt**: Remain flexible and adaptable in your approach to achieving your financial goals. Recognize that setbacks and challenges are a natural part of the journey, and be willing to adjust your plans as needed. Focus on finding solutions rather than dwelling on problems, and maintain a growth mindset that embraces learning and improvement.

By effectively managing your emotions and staying motivated, you can overcome obstacles, stay focused on your financial goals, and ultimately achieve greater success and fulfillment in your life. Remember to be patient and compassionate with yourself, and celebrate the progress you've made along the way.

# Chapter 7

# The seduction of status

The seduction of status is a powerful force that can exert a significant influence on individuals' behaviors, choices, and perceptions, particularly in the realm of wealth accumulation. Status represents one's social standing, prestige, and recognition within a community or society, and it often becomes intertwined with notions of success, power, and worthiness.

The allure of status can manifest in various ways, tempting individuals to prioritize external validation and recognition over intrinsic values and personal fulfillment. Here are some of the ways in which the seduction of status can manifest:

1.    **Materialism and Conspicuous Consumption**: The pursuit of status often leads individuals to engage in conspicuous consumption, where the acquisition and display of luxury goods and possessions serve as symbols of wealth and social status. This conspicuous consumption not only drains financial resources but also perpetuates a cycle of comparison and competition, where individuals feel compelled to keep up with others' materialistic displays to maintain their perceived status.

2. **Social Comparison and Envy**: The seduction of status fuels social comparison and envy, as individuals constantly measure themselves against others in terms of wealth, possessions, achievements, and lifestyles. This comparison mindset can breed feelings of inadequacy, insecurity, and discontent, as individuals strive to attain or surpass the status

of their peers, often at the expense of their own well-being and financial stability.

3. **Ego and Self-Validation**: Status can become intertwined with individuals' sense of self-worth and identity, leading to ego-driven behaviors and a relentless pursuit of external validation. The seduction of status can inflate individuals' egos, fostering a sense of superiority, entitlement, and narcissism that blinds them to the true sources of fulfillment and meaning in life.

4. **Financial Risk-Taking and Overextension**: In the quest for status, individuals may be tempted to take on excessive financial risks or overextend themselves financially in pursuit of high-status symbols such as luxury homes, cars, or memberships. This can lead to financial instability, debt accumulation, and stress, as individuals prioritize the appearance of wealth and status over long-term financial security and well-being.

5. **Emotional and Psychological Toll**: The seduction of status can exact a toll on individuals' emotional and psychological well-being, fueling anxiety, depression, and a sense of emptiness or disillusionment. Despite outward appearances of success and status, individuals may struggle with feelings of inadequacy, loneliness, and disconnection from their authentic selves, as they chase external validation and approval.

In essence, the seduction of status represents a complex interplay of societal norms, cultural influences, and individual psychology that can profoundly impact individuals' financial decisions and overall well-being. Recognizing the seductive allure of status and cultivating a mindset grounded in authenticity, humility, and intrinsic values can help individuals navigate the complexities of wealth accumulation with integrity, mindfulness, and a sense of purpose.

# CHAPTER 8

# The Art of contentment

The art of contentment is a timeless practice that involves finding satisfaction and peace within oneself, independent of external circumstances or material possessions. It is about embracing a mindset of gratitude, acceptance, and fulfillment in the present moment, rather than constantly striving for more or comparing oneself to others.

At its core, the art of contentment is about recognizing and appreciating the abundance that exists in one's life, regardless of one's financial situation or social status. It involves cultivating an attitude of gratitude for the simple pleasures and blessings that surround us, from the warmth of the sun on a clear day to the laughter of loved ones gathered around a table.

Contentment also entails accepting and embracing life's inevitable ups and downs with equanimity and grace. It is about recognizing that challenges and setbacks are a natural part of the human experience and viewing them as opportunities for growth, learning, and resilience. Rather than resisting or resenting difficulties, contentment encourages individuals to approach them with curiosity, compassion, and a sense of inner strength.

Moreover, the art of contentment involves letting go of the constant need for external validation and approval and instead finding validation from within. It is about recognizing one's inherent worth and value as a human being, independent of achievements, possessions, or social status. By cultivating self-compassion and self-acceptance, individuals can experience a deep sense of contentment and inner peace that transcends the fleeting highs and lows of external circumstances.

In the context of wealth accumulation, the art of contentment offers a powerful antidote to the seductive allure of status and materialism. Rather than measuring success solely by financial metrics or comparing oneself to others, individuals practicing contentment focus on aligning their financial goals with their values, priorities, and aspirations. They recognize that true wealth is not just about accumulating possessions or achieving external markers of success but about living a life of meaning, purpose, and fulfillment.

In summary, the art of contentment is a profound practice that invites individuals to cultivate gratitude, acceptance, and inner peace in their lives. By embracing contentment, individuals can experience greater satisfaction, resilience, and well-being, regardless of their external circumstances or financial status. It is a timeless art that offers profound wisdom and guidance in the pursuit of a rich and fulfilling life.

# CONCLUSION

In conclusion, I want to express my heartfelt gratitude for taking this journey with me. I hope that along the way, you've discovered valuable insights and lessons about the intertwining paths of wealth and happiness. May these learnings serve as guiding lights as you navigate the complexities of life, finances, and personal fulfillment.

As you continue on your journey, I encourage you to take what you've learned and weave it into the fabric of your existence. Let the wisdom gained from our exploration empower you to cultivate a life filled with love, abundance, and purpose. Remember to cherish every moment, celebrate your victories, and embrace the challenges as opportunities for growth.

With warmest wishes for a future brimming with joy, success, and fulfillment, I bid you farewell. May your path be illuminated by love, and may you always find peace and contentment along the way. Thank you for sharing this journey with me, and may your days ahead be filled with boundless blessings and endless possibilities. Best wishes on your continued journey of wealth and happiness.

# ABOUT THE AUTHOR

Oliver George is a seasoned financial advisor, entrepreneur, and author dedicated to empowering individuals to achieve financial freedom and fulfillment. With over two decades of experience in the financial industry, Oliver has earned a reputation for his expertise in wealth management, investment strategies, and personal finance.

As a passionate advocate for financial literacy and empowerment, Oliver has dedicated his career to helping people take control of their finances, build wealth, and create the lives they desire. Through his work as a financial advisor, Oliver has guided countless individuals and families on their journey towards financial success, providing personalized guidance and strategies tailored to their unique goals and circumstances.

In addition to his work as a financial advisor, Oliver is also an accomplished author, with several best-selling books on personal finance and wealth management to his name. His writing is known for its clarity, practicality, and actionable insights, making complex financial concepts accessible to readers of all backgrounds.

Oliver's mission is to demystify the world of finance and empower individuals to make informed decisions about their money, ultimately leading to greater financial stability, security, and peace of mind. Through his books, seminars, and online courses, Oliver continues to inspire and educate people around the world to take control of their financial futures and live life on their own terms.